All serious daring starts from within.

— *Eudora Welty,*
Novelist and
short story writer

For Mom, Dad,
Katie, and Eric

Girls Who Grew Up Great

A Book of
Encouragement
for Girls
About Amazing Women
Who Dared to Dream

Gwendolyn Gray

Blue Mountain Press ™
Boulder, Colorado

Library of Congress Catalog Card Number: 2003011049
ISBN: 0-88396-752-9

ACKNOWLEDGMENTS appear on page 64.

Certain trademarks are used under license.

Manufactured in the United States of America.

Second Printing: 2004

 This book is printed on recycled paper.

This book is printed on fine quality, laid embossed, 80 lb. paper. This paper has been specially produced to be acid free (neutral pH) and contains no groundwood or unbleached pulp. It conforms with all the requirements of the American National Standards Institute, Inc., so as to ensure that this book will last and be enjoyed by future generations.

Library of Congress Cataloging-in-Publication Data

Gray, Gwendolyn, 1976-
Girls who grew up great : a book of encouragement for girls about amazing women who dared to dream / Gwendolyn Gray.
      p. cm.
      ISBN 0-88396-752-9 (softcover : alk. paper)
1. Girls—Biography. 2. Women—Biography. 3. Encouragement. I. Title.

CT3205.G73 2003
920.72—dc21

2003011049
CIP

Blue Mountain Arts, Inc.
P.O. Box 4549, Boulder, Colorado 80306

Contents

There is a great line of women stretching out behind you into the past, and you have to seek them out and find them in yourself and be conscious of them.

— *Doris Lessing,*
British novelist

Listen and learn from those who have gone before you — the great women of the past. In their stories, you will find keys that will help you unlock your true potential. But you must learn to listen to them with your heart.

— *Rosalind Andrews-Worthy,*
Director of an AIDS education program

Hey, Girls! As you may have noticed already, this book has a message just for you:

There are no limits to what you can do!

Now, I know that you know that, but sometimes it's hard to remember it — to stay in touch with your hopes and dreams — when you're busy with the everyday things happening on this roller coaster we call life. So it is my hope that the *amazing women* featured in this book will help remind you that it's possible to make a difference in the world, in any and all of the ways you want to.

The women featured here — some you've probably heard of and a lot you probably haven't — represent a teeny tiny portion of all the *remarkable* women in the world who deserve recognition for their achievements. But these few were specially chosen to inspire you to let your imagination *fly free* and to *dare to dream*.

Call them what you want — trailblazers, groundbreakers, revolutionaries, or pioneers — these women all have at least one thing in common: *They paved the way for you!* When the odds were against them, they kept trying and showed the world that *women can do anything*. So make use of the paths they've forged and take the wonderful opportunities that are offered to you. I am sure they would want you to hear their stories, and I *know* they would want to hear your amazing stories of the achievements that *you* are sure to make as you *grow up great!*

— Gwendolyn Gray

Thumbprint

On the pad of my thumb
are whorls, whirls, wheels
in a unique design:
mine alone.
What a treasure to own!
My own flesh, my own feelings.
No other, however grand or base,
can ever contain the same.
My signature,
thumbing the pages of my time.
My universe key,
my singularity.
Impress, implant,
I am myself,
of all my atom parts I am the sum.
And out of my blood and my brain
I make my own interior weather,
my own sun and rain.
Imprint my mark upon the world
whatever I shall become.

— Eve Merriam,
Poet, playwright,
director, and lecturer

Making Your Mark

Maria Montessori
1870–1952

Against her parents' wishes, Maria Montessori decided to attend school, eventually becoming the first woman in Italy to receive a medical degree when she graduated from the University of Rome in 1896. After beginning her work as a physician, she immediately developed an interest in how children learn. She began working with a group of mentally disabled children who quickly and remarkably progressed under her care. In 1907, she opened the Children's House in a rundown section of Rome and began working with and observing the children there. She noticed that they had a natural craving to learn. Based on this discovery, she developed a method of education in which adults direct a child's self-learning process. Soon people were coming from all over to see the amazing progress Maria's students were making. She also taught in the United States, and after fleeing Italy's fascist movement, she taught in Spain, in the Netherlands, and in India. The Montessori method of education is still used in many places today.

 STAR QUALITIES: Innovative, Compassionate, Generous

To Dark Eyes Dreaming

Dreams go fast and far
   these days.
They go by rocket thrust.
They go arrayed
   in lights
      or in the dust of stars.
Dreams, these days,
   go fast and far.
Dreams are young, these days,
   or very old,
They can be black,
   or blue or gold.
They need no special charts,
   nor any fuel.
It seems, only one rule applies,
   to all our dreams —
They will not fly except in open sky.
   A fenced-in dream
      will die.

— Zilpha Keatley Snyder,
Poet and author
of children's books

Reaching for the Stars

Jerrie Cobb
1931-

In 1960, an accomplished American airplane pilot named Jerrie Cobb began taking the examinations required to become an astronaut. She passed every one of the grueling physical and psychological tests required to join the space program with outstanding results. Thirteen other women were deemed equally qualified and were eager to become astronauts, too. But suddenly Jerrie and the other women were barred from advancing through the astronaut program. Jerrie went to Congress to testify on behalf of the women denied the opportunity to become astronauts. She fought hard to convince the U.S. government and NASA to allow women to join the space program, yet they were denied participation in the program simply because they were women.

STAR QUALITIES: Patient, Charismatic, Driven

Sally Ride
1951-

It was not until 1983 that Sally Ride broke this difficult barrier for women, becoming the first American woman to go into space. She has also founded The Sally Ride Science Club to encourage and support girls who are interested in science, math, and technology.

STAR QUALITIES: Strong, Intelligent, Trailblazing

Performing with Passion

Clara Schumann
1819-1896

After her mother and father divorced, little Clara Wieck of Leipzig, Germany, withdrew into unhappiness and hardly spoke or interacted with anyone. As a result, she was thought to be hearing impaired. Then, at the age of five, when her father began giving her piano lessons, it became clear that she could read and hear music just fine. In fact, it wasn't long before she could listen to a musical piece only once and then play it perfectly on the piano. Clara gave her first concert when she was nine, and by age 11 had composed four pieces of music. When she was very young, Clara fell in love with one of her father's students, Robert Schumann, who had a talent for composing music. She helped promote his compositions by playing them to her fans. They eventually married and Clara, at Robert's request, stopped performing. Her frequent pregnancies — eight children in 10 years — also prevented her from playing. When she returned to touring, Robert found it difficult to deal with Clara's fame and success. After being plagued by depression, he was committed to a mental institution and died in 1854. Clara made the best of her single-parent status by continuing to play piano concerts to support her family. She had an amazingly long career as a pianist and composer, and she helped many previously unknown composers reach a legendary status, including her husband.

 STAR QUALITIES: Talented, Persevering, Self-Sufficient

If you don't like the way the world is, you change it. You have an obligation to change it. You just do it one step at a time.

— Marian Wright Edelman,
Founder of Children's Defense Fund

One can never consent to creep when one feels an impulse to soar.

— Helen Keller,
Blind and deaf author and lecturer

Independence is happiness.

— Susan B. Anthony,
Reformer and suffragette

Standing Up (or Staying Put) for What You Know Is Right

Rosa Parks
1913-

In 1955, in Montgomery, Alabama and throughout the South, buses had separate sections for African-American and white passengers. Blacks were only allowed to sit in the white sections if no white person needed the seat. Rosa Parks made a huge impact on history when she refused to give up one such bus seat to a white man. She was arrested for not complying with the rules, but her courage inspired others to boycott the Montgomery bus system. Her insistence to fight for what she knew was right is considered one of the most important steppingstones of the civil rights movement, which eventually won many rights and improvements for African-Americans in the United States.

 STAR QUALITIES: Proud, Courageous, Dignified

Finding Comfort in Your Talent

Frida Kahlo
1907–1954

Born outside of Mexico City, Frida Kahlo lived a life full of difficulties and physical pain that she coped with and expressed through her painting. When she was seven, she contracted polio, which damaged her right foot and leg. Then, when she was a young teenager, she was involved in a terrible bus accident that left her disabled for the rest of her life. She began painting during the recovery from this accident, and many of her most famous works were painted while lying flat on her back, confined to her bed. Her paintings are intensely personal and brightly colored, directly conveying her emotional and physical pains and pleasures. Frida also had a turbulent relationship with her husband, artist Diego Rivera, and was unable to bear children — facts that are also reflected in her paintings. Frida was politically active and became a powerful icon of nationality for Mexican men and women. She is known as one of the most spirited and talented artists to ever emerge from Mexico.

 STAR QUALITIES: Imaginative, Artistic, Intense

Sticking with It

Dame Margot Fonteyn
1919-1991

Born in England as Peggy Hookham, this talented
dancer became the Royal Ballet's prima ballerina
under the stage name Margot Fonteyn. She was
known for her excellent musicality and technical
aptitude. In 1962, the famous Russian dancer,
Rudolf Nureyev, joined her on stage for several
incredible performances, and they became one of
the most famous ballet duos in history. Margot
had a remarkably long career for a ballerina,
dancing and performing into her late fifties.

 STAR QUALITIES: Elegant,
Enduring, Dynamic

It is never too late to be what you might have been.

— George Eliot (Mary Ann Evans),
British novelist

Expressing Yourself

Natalia Makarova
1940-

On a whim, at age 13, Natalia Makarova joined the Vaganova School of Ballet in her hometown of Leningrad in the Soviet Union. After quickly rising to the position of principal dancer, Natalia eventually became tired of performing the same traditional roles of classical ballet. She learned about the creative freedom that dancers in other countries were allowed, and this inspired her to leave the Soviet Union. As punishment, the Soviet government erased her name from the country's official records, including all books on ballet and encyclopedias! Yet Natalia went on to prove herself across the world as one of the greatest ballet dancers of all time. She was eventually invited to return to the Soviet Union and danced to sold-out crowds in her homeland.

 STAR QUALITIES: Independent, Graceful, Ambitious

Everything I have achieved came through my own accomplishments. Nobody helped me.... Basically I had to fight for what I got.

— Natalia Makarova,
Ballet dancer

I wear many blues

I am blue
Not just one blue...
Many blues
The skin I wear is the sea
The nose I wear is royal blue
The hair I wear is light blue
The mouth I have is dark blue
The ears I wear are bird blue
So short am I
Short and blue
A big fat blueberry is what I am
Roly and poly
I am the only blue one
Alone
Scared
With no one to talk to
People would eat me if only they could
Everyone stares at my bluish hair
And the big blue shoes I wear
I know I'm quite different but
That's on the outside
And not on the in
I feel like a parrot among a bunch of pigeons
The fashions will change
But not me, no not me
I am blue

— Cara Rabin,
     Poet

Setting a Style
All Your Own

Coco Chanel
1883-1971

After her mother died and her father abandoned her, the young French girl named Gabrielle Chanel was left to grow up in an orphanage and later at a convent-run boarding school. As a young woman, Gabrielle worked with her aunt as an assistant in a clothing and fabric shop. She waited on customers and quickly earned a reputation for her skillful sewing and alterations. To earn money on the side, she also sang in nightclubs, where she acquired the nickname Coco. Gaining entrance into the upper-class social scene, Coco observed the elaborate styles flaunted by these fashionable women. But being active and slim, Coco did not conform to these styles; instead she wore simple and comfortable outfits — sometimes even pants and shirts borrowed from boyfriends. She began designing minimally decorated, elegant hats, which quickly gained popularity. Soon she was running a very successful fashion house, and her designs took off during World War I. She also created a perfume, simply called Chanel No. 5, that became all the rage. Her business eventually grew into a fashion empire that employed over 3,000 people, and her designs have surfaced in an incredible number of revivals throughout the years. She is admired for making high fashion available to working women and for the amazing endurance of her name in the fashion industry.

STAR QUALITIES: Stylish, Hardworking, Tasteful

Finding a Solution

Bette Nesmith Graham
1924–1980

Bette Nesmith Graham was a 17-year-old single mother
working in a secretarial job in Dallas, Texas, when she
encountered one particularly annoying problem: The
electric typewriters supplied at the time made it difficult
to erase any errors she might make while typing. Drawing
inspiration from watching painters simply paint over their
mistakes, she began using a thin white paint to cover
her typos. She taught herself the chemistry principles
needed to perfect her formula, created batches of it
in her kitchen, and eventually applied for a patent. Her
"Liquid Paper" was quickly in high demand. In 1979,
Bette was able to sell her company, which had grown
to an enterprise of 200 employees, to the Gillette
Corporation for $47.5 million!

 STAR QUALITIES: Resourceful,
Enterprising, Clever

Improving the World

Margaret Knight
1838-1914

Margaret, or "Mattie," Knight was always interested in figuring out how mechanisms worked and how to build things, which at the time was considered strange for a girl. But her curiosity was put to good use when she was only 12. She observed a terrible accident in the New Hampshire mill where she worked when a woman was seriously injured by a malfunctioning loom. Horrified, she devised a way for a loom to automatically shut down the moment it malfunctioned. Then, while working at a paper bag company, she invented a machine that could cut, fold, and paste a paper bag together without human help — and the bags were sturdier and flat-bottomed (like the grocery bags we still use today). Though she had to fight in court against a man who falsely claimed that he invented the bag-folding machine, she was finally granted a patent for her work. Her invention ultimately earned Mattie $50,000. She went on to create many more useful inventions and taught herself about patent law and business negotiating, making her one of the most admired female inventors of all time.

 STAR QUALITIES: Creative, Inventive, Assertive

Adults often don't understand a lot of things about kids. We often crush some of the most precious things. But if you can hold on to your curiosity, you'll have a better chance of finding yourself: who you are, what you want, and what you want to be — right now, tomorrow, ten years from now, forever.

— Lauren Hutton,
Model and actress

Taking Matters into Your Own Hands

Sybil Ludington
1761-1839

You've probably read about an important figure in the Revolutionary War named Paul Revere, who in 1775 made a famous ride the night before the Battle of Lexington to warn colonists of the approaching British forces. What most of us never learn in history class is that, in 1777, a 16-year-old girl rode twice the distance as Paul Revere in an almost identical situation. Young Sybil Ludington raced from town to town, alerting New York and Connecticut colonists that the British had begun an attack on Danbury, Connecticut. Amazingly, she summoned enough volunteers to fight off the redcoats the next day.

 STAR QUALITIES: Selfless, Loyal, Tireless

The time when you need to do something is when no one else is willing to do it, when people are saying it can't be done.

— Mary Frances Berry,
Chairperson of U.S. Commission on Civil Rights

Always try to show people the respect you hope they'll show you. And help them with the things that are hardest for them as you would hope they'd help you.

— Sheryl Swoopes,
WNBA basketball player

Giving All You've Got

Maggie Lena Walker
1867–1934

After her early teaching career in Richmond, Virginia, Maggie Lena Walker created a juvenile division that nurtured and taught children for one of her community's charitable organizations. She was then appointed secretary of the board for another group of organizations that sought to offer African-Americans easier access to loans. Here Maggie worked to encourage independence for the black community and urged women to participate in the business world. She spent time practicing accounting and learning about business and, at age 27, became the first female bank president in the United States. As you might imagine, for a black woman to take on such an important position in the South in 1903 was highly uncommon. Under Maggie's management, St. Luke Penny Saving Bank prospered, even through the Great Depression — and it continues to operate today. Somehow, Maggie also found time to participate in many other community organizations that promoted the advancement of African-Americans in society, including the National Association of Colored Women and the National Association for the Advancement of Colored People.

 STAR QUALITIES: Foresighted, Optimistic, Generous

That's what being young is all about. You have the courage and the daring to think that you can make a difference.

— Ruby Dee,
Actress

Once you know what is right and wrong, you must stand up for your beliefs. When someone is doing the wrong thing, it is time to speak out. This world needs more people with the courage to act on their beliefs. Don't be afraid to speak against injustice. Even if you are picked on for taking a stand and for having high ideals, you must persevere.

— Rebecca Lobo,
WNBA basketball player

Speaking Out Against Wrongs

Dorothea Lynde Dix
1802–1887

By the age of 14, Dorothea Lynde Dix had educated herself and opened a school for small children in Worcester, Massachusetts. By 1832, she had published a science textbook and several devotional books for schoolchildren. When her health began to fail, however, she was unable to continue teaching. Dorothea was 39 when she was invited to lead a Sunday school class for women at the local jail. There she was appalled to discover that mentally ill women were locked up with criminals and living in filthy, horrible conditions. Dorothea went into action, investigating every jail in Massachusetts and submitting her discoveries about the atrocious treatment of mentally ill men and women to the legislature. She insisted that mentally ill patients be housed and cared for in separate institutions from criminals. The legislature responded by allocating money to create state facilities for the proper care of the mentally ill. She was able to successfully take her crusade to several different states and Canada and also worked in Europe to reform prisons and hospitals. During the Civil War, she was recruited as superintendent of the nurses for the Union Army. She hired and trained thousands of nurses to provide service to the army and greatly contributed to the acceptance of women in the healthcare profession.

 STAR QUALITIES: Outspoken, Humanitarian, Pioneering

Going to Extraordinary Measures

Deborah Sampson
(a.k.a. Robert Shurtleff)
1760-1827

Deborah Sampson was the first woman to enlist in the American armed forces. In order to participate as a soldier in the Revolutionary War, she disguised herself as a male and registered using the name Robert Shurtleff. She served in the 4th Massachusetts Regiment and, during one battle, was shot in the leg. In order to keep her identity hidden, she tended to the wound herself. Eventually, her gender was discovered and she was honorably discharged from the army. She was awarded a government pension and toured New England lecturing about her experiences in the war.

 STAR QUALITIES: Daring, Adventurous, Individualistic

Adventure is worthwhile in itself.

— Amelia Earhart,
Aviator

Paving Your Own Way

Miranda Stuart
(a.k.a. Dr. James Barry)
1795-1865

In the 1800's in Britain, women were not permitted to practice medicine. This did not stop Miranda Stuart. While still a teenager, she concealed her gender, renamed herself James Barry, and began taking classes at the prestigious University of Edinburgh in Scotland. Her disguise worked. She became a doctor and eventually became the highest-ranking surgeon in the British army. She traveled quite extensively throughout the world and was known for her courage and talent. Her identity was not discovered until her death in 1865.

 STAR QUALITIES: Resolute, Intelligent, Unconventional

Stealing the Show

Sarah Bernhardt
1844-1923

Though Sarah Bernhardt's life was often known to be as dramatic as the roles she played on stage, her fiery personality led her to a level of success that helped open doors for other women in theater. Born in Paris as Rosine Bernard, she was quite young when she realized her passion for acting. She enrolled in the Conservatoire, France's national theater school, when was she was just 16. It was not long before Sarah was performing for local theaters and earning great praise for her graceful movements and clear voice. She gained overwhelming popularity and was dubbed the Divine Sarah. She formed her own theater company that traveled around the world playing to countless admiring audiences. With complete reign over her company, Sarah was free to embrace new roles, including male roles that women did not typically get to play. When a knee injury required that her leg be amputated in 1915, she continued acting by altering the roles so that she could be seated. Sarah also was talented at painting and sculpting, writing poems and plays, and managing other theater companies in Paris. Though she was thought to be rather eccentric, sometimes keeping animals like lions in her home and throwing wild parties, her command of the stage earned her a reputation as a world-class actress.

 STAR QUALITIES: Lively, Multitalented, Spirited

Great necessities call out great virtues.

— Abigail Adams,
Former first lady

Nothing is impossible to a valiant heart.

— Jeanne D'Albret,
Queen of Navarre, 1555–1572

How wonderful it is that nobody need wait a single moment before starting to improve the world.

— Anne Frank,
German Jewish diarist

Making a Difference

Bernadette Devlin McAliskey
1947-

While Bernadette Devlin was attending school at Queen's University in Northern Ireland, she participated in a civil rights rally in which she witnessed a young man being beaten by the police. This infuriated her and caused her to begin actively organizing groups to fight for equality and justice in Northern Ireland. She became a hero to many people and was elected as the youngest woman ever to sit in British parliament. At 21 years old, she captivated parliament with her passionate speeches about problems in Northern Ireland. She continued her activism back home, and once spent four months in prison as a result. When she was released, she continued to speak for the Irish Catholic cause amidst the Catholic and Protestant tensions in Northern Ireland. A group of Protestant terrorists broke into her home one morning and shot Bernadette 14 times. They barely missed hitting her heart, and Bernadette miraculously survived. Amazingly, this attack did not stop her efforts. She is still working for her cause today.

STAR QUALITIES: Passionate, Dedicated, Fearless

Planting the Seeds of Tomorrow

Wangari Maathai
1940-

After completing her master's degree in science on a scholarship to the United States, Wangari Maathai returned to her homeland of Kenya, bringing back her knowledge and a desire to make a difference in her country. She soon became the first Kenyan woman to receive a doctorate from the University of Nairobi, where she was made professor and appointed head of the Anatomy Department. After marrying a member of the Kenyan Parliament, she worked in her husband's district to improve conditions for women and the poor. She decided to run for parliament, but was forced to give up her campaign and was not allowed to return to her post at the university because her male colleagues disapproved of a woman taking on such responsibilities. Later, after realizing that deforestation in Kenya was sure to lead to human and environmental disaster, she launched a new project by planting trees in a public park. She traveled through Kenya, teaching village women how to plant trees and cultivate tree seedlings. Her enthusiasm spread, and since 1977, over 15 million trees have been planted throughout Africa. Wangari continues to fight for the equal treatment and rights of all Kenyan people. Her activism once caused her to be beaten unconscious by the police. Even this has not stopped her astounding efforts to protect the rights of the environment, women, and all humans.

STAR QUALITIES: Dauntless, Untiring, Farsighted

I am doing something I learned early to do, I am
paying attention to small beauties,
whatever I have — as if it were our duty to
find things to love, to bind ourselves to this world.

— Sharon Olds,
Poet

*T*o be surrounded by beautiful things has much
influence upon the human creature: to make beautiful
things has more.

— Margaret Fuller,
Social reformer and author

Telling It How It Is

Murasaki Shikibu
c.978–1015

We do not know this important woman's real name, but she went by Lady Murasaki, the name of a character from her famous novel, *The Tale of Genji*. This book made an unforgettable mark on history because it is believed to be the world's first novel. Known also as one of the world's greatest novels, Murasaki's story displays her remarkable awareness of human emotions, her love of nature and beauty, and her extensive knowledge in many subjects. *The Tale of Genji* skillfully captures images from the time in which Murasaki lived and has had a tremendous influence on Japanese and world culture.

 STAR QUALITIES: Observant, Expressive, Influential

Surfboard Life

I'm riding on a surfboard life
someone gave me
a while ago I started out
in the middle of some wavy water
I've been surfing ever since
I fall off
a wave hits me from behind
then there I go
back on that surfing thing
I live on
no land is in sight
the streams of water
spray around me
I balance
the crest is below me
I can't be stopped now

— Julie O'Callaghan,
Poet

Exercising All Your Potential

Babe Didrikson Zaharias
1914–1956

Right from the start, Mildred Didrikson, nicknamed "Babe" after the sports hero Babe Ruth, started demonstrating rare athletic abilities. She could beat all the boys and girls she competed against in her Texas hometown at any sport. She competed in sports throughout high school and eventually was hired to play basketball for an insurance company out of Dallas, quickly becoming the leader of the team. In 1932, she entered the Amateur Athletic Union as a track-and-field contestant and won six events, broke four women's world records, and won a team championship as a one-woman team! Next she competed at the Olympics, winning gold medals in track-and-field events and again breaking world records. Seeing little opportunity to support herself in amateur sports, she turned her attentions to golf. Three years later, she won the Texas Women's Amateur Championship, and won many other tournaments that followed. She helped establish the Ladies Professional Golf Association. She is remembered as one of the greatest athletes of all time and is recognized for helping to make the world of sports more accessible to women.

STAR QUALITIES: Determined, Unrelenting, Positive

Girls Incorporated
Girls' Bill of Rights

⋄ *Girls have the right to be themselves and to resist gender stereotypes.*

⋄ *Girls have the right to express themselves with originality and enthusiasm.*

⋄ *Girls have the right to take risks, to strive freely, and to take pride in success.*

⋄ *Girls have the right to accept and appreciate their bodies.*

⋄ *Girls have the right to have confidence in themselves and to be safe in the world.*

⋄ *Girls have the right to prepare for interesting work and economic independence.*

Fighting for Fairness

Angelina Grimké
1805–1879

Sarah Moore Grimké
1792–1873

These sisters are credited as the first women to speak publicly against slavery, and they are among the first American women to push for women's equality. Born in Charleston, South Carolina, the girls were brought up in a well-to-do slaveholding family. As they matured, they became deeply opposed to slavery and eventually left the South, moving to Philadelphia to become Quakers and to speak out against slavery. Angelina called on women, in particular, to oppose slavery and condemned the use of the messages in the Bible as justification for slavery. Soon they were making public appearances and expressing their strong beliefs to men and women all over the North. As a result, the sisters were criticized as "unwomanly" and were publicly denounced for continuing their crusade against slavery. The pair responded by writing pamphlets asserting the rights of women to free speech and participation in the formation of laws. Despite the challenges they faced, the Grimké sisters continued to write and speak against slavery, and the rest of their careers were spent as teachers and enthusiasts of progressive causes.

 STAR QUALITIES: Freethinking, Open-minded, Persuasive

Discovering the Important Things in Life

Rosalind Franklin
1920-1958

By the age of 15, Rosalind Franklin already knew that she wanted to become a scientist. When she was old enough to attend college, she applied to Cambridge University and was granted admission. Her father, however, did not approve of women attending university, and he refused to pay her tuition. Fortunately, Rosalind's mother stood by her side and her aunt offered to pay for the education. After obtaining her Ph.D. at Cambridge, she began experimenting with how to use x-rays to create photographic images of molecules. When she joined a team of scientists at King's College, she was assigned the project of trying to discover the structure of deoxyribonucleic acid, or DNA, the basic genetic material of all living things. The peer who was also assigned to the project, Maurice Wilkins, misunderstood their relationship and assumed that Rosalind was merely his assistant. When Rosalind uncovered the keys to understanding DNA's "double-helix" structure by using her skills in creating x-ray photographic images, Maurice gave her data, without her consent or knowledge, to two men at Cambridge University who then used it to pull ahead in the race for discovering the structure of DNA. The men won the Nobel Prize for the discovery and gave no credit to Rosalind. Though she never received proper recognition, it is now known that her research was essential to this very important discovery. Rosalind spent the rest of her life continuing with research and making important scientific findings.

STAR QUALITIES: Unselfish, Diligent, Astute

Wanda Gág

When Father died, the neighbors told her,
"Quit school, Wanda. Go to work."
With seven children's mouths to fill,
her mother sorely needed help,
for she was frail and gravely ill.

No. Wanda wouldn't quit.
She stayed in school,
then after class she dusted, swept,
and cooked a brothy stew.
She patched and mended piles of clothes,
washed and did the ironing, too.

Later while the whole house slept,
though weary,
Wanda dipped her pen in ink,
and drew pictures she could sell to magazines.
Her postcards, place cards,
and small bookmarks all sold well,
as did her cards for holidays.
She kept a record of each sale
and every night toiled late again.
She finished school — her siblings, too! —
supported by her artist's pen.

— Ann Whitford Paul,
Poet

Making a Name for Yourself

Rosa Bonheur
1822-1899

Rosa Bonheur was just a young girl when her mother died. Her father, a talented but unappreciated painter, was barely able to support her and her three siblings by giving drawing lessons to earn money. He knew that his daughter wanted to be an artist and had natural ability — she skillfully drew pictures of animals on the bedroom walls — but he discouraged her because he knew how difficult it was to make a living as an artist. But when Rosa was expelled from school for unruly behavior, her father gave in and began to formally train her in art. Since the family lived in Paris, he sent her on visits to the nearby Louvre, one of the world's most famous art museums, where she could study and copy the paintings of the masters. Before long, she was able to imitate them almost perfectly. Rosa rediscovered her love for animals by going out into fields to paint livestock. Soon Rosa's animal paintings were shown at the Paris Salon, and they ultimately soared in popularity. Among her paintings, *The Horse Fair* and *Plowing in the Nivernais* were immediately recognized as works of genius and still hang in famous museums today, as do many of her other works. Her talents earned her the privilege of being the first woman to receive the medal of the French Legion of Honor. She was able to support herself and help her family escape poverty. Her father became the director of the government school of design, and when he died, she took over his position.

 STAR QUALITIES: Decisive, Persistent, Original

Girls Can, Too!

Tony said: "Boys are better!
    They can...
        whack a ball,
        ride a bike with one hand,
        leap off a wall."

I just listened
    and when he was through,
I laughed and said:

    "Oh, yeah! Well, girls can, too!"

Then I leaped off the wall
    and rode away
With his 200 baseball cards
    I won that day.

— Lee Bennett Hopkins,
Poet, anthologist, and teacher

Proving Yourself
to the World

Billy Jean King
1943-

Billy Jean King, a sports-lover from a very young age, was a star athlete at Los Angeles State College, yet she found she was not eligible for scholarships because she was a woman. She also found that the tournaments she competed in and won paid less prize money to women than to men. Billy Jean set out to draw attention to this unfair treatment of women in athletics. While working toward this goal, she broke every previous professional tennis record for women. She scored a win for all women after she took on a challenge from tennis pro Bobby Riggs, who asserted that a female tennis player could never be as good as a male. It was settled in their televised 1973 match when she beat him in three straight sets. This was just one of the battles she fought and won in her struggle to advocate women's recognition and equal pay in sports. She founded the Women's Tennis Association and the Women's Sport Foundation, and she published *WomenSport*, a magazine that covered stories regarding women athletes and their progress in the world of sports.

STAR QUALITIES: Competitive,
Confident, Aggressive

Standing Your Ground

Queen Boudica
c.25-62

Boudica was born into a royal family in the Celtic tribe called the Iceni, who lived in the area we now know as Norfolk, England. She married her tribe's wealthy king, Prasutagus, and they had two daughters together. Even though invading Romans controlled the region at the time, Prasutagus decreed that when he died, Boudica would take over the throne. However, when he passed away in the year 60, the Romans refused to allow Boudica to rule. They began to pillage and destroy the kingdom and physically harmed Boudica and her two daughters. The rightful queen became enraged. She recruited an army of approximately 120,000 soldiers from her own tribe and another nearby tribe and planned a rebellion. When she knew the Roman leaders were busy with other affairs in Wales, she led an attack against the Roman settlements. Her fearless army was able to severely devastate the Romans, but when the remaining Roman forces returned from Wales, they thwarted Boudica's army. Nevertheless, Queen Boudica's legacy as a warrior and a great leader has survived all these long years, evidence of the serious threat she posed to the Romans and a testament to her power and the force of her will.

 STAR QUALITIES: Self-motivated, Commanding, Legendary

Leading the Way Together

Trung Trac
c.42

Trung Nhi
c.42

Trung Trac and Trung Nhi were daughters of an artistocratic family in Vietnam, which had been under the control of China for over a hundred years. In 39 A.D., a Chinese general killed Trung Trac's husband, a powerful Vietnamese nobleman, and assaulted the two sisters. In response, the sisters decided to lead a revolt against the Chinese. Together, they raised an army of 80,000 people led largely by female generals, trained them to fight, and drove the Chinese out of Vietnam. Trung Nhi proved to be a powerful warrior and Trung Trac an influential leader. Both were chosen by the people as new rulers after the victory. The success and power they shared became legendary. Even though the Chinese took control of Vietnam again not long after the revolt, some people believe that the nation of Vietnam would not exist today had Trung Trac and Trung Nhi not stood up to the Chinese. You can still find temples in Vietnam that honor the two sisters and a national holiday is dedicated to their memory.

 STAR QUALITIES: United, Forceful, Valiant

Making the World a Better Place

Rachel Carson
1907–1964

As Rachel Carson grew up in Pennsylvania, she discovered a love for nature and being outdoors. She also loved reading and writing, so she entered college as an English major but switched to science after taking a biology class that absolutely fascinated her. She eventually realized that she could combine her two talents, and in 1951 she published a bestselling book entitled *The Sea Around Us*. In 1958, a friend sent Rachel a letter complaining that she noticed a large number of birds had died after a pesticide called DDT was sprayed on plants. Rachel decided to study the effects of chemicals like DDT, and she soon discovered that they damaged the environment, killing or harming thousands of plants and animals. She wrote articles about her findings, but no one would publish her work because it was sure to cause controversy with pesticide companies. So Rachel wrote an entire book on the topic, entitled *Silent Spring*. The book was immediately attacked by the chemical industry, but no matter how hard they tried, they could not find any flaws in her research or arguments. In response, the U.S. government changed its policies on pesticides and banned the use of DDT. Before Rachel's famous book, people did not give much thought to how human progress affects the environment. It is widely believed that she started the environmental protection movement.

 STAR QUALITIES: Caring, Sincere, Curious

Where are those songs?

Mother always said
sing child sing
make a song
and sing
beat out your own rhythms
the rhythms of your life
but make the song soulful
and make life
sing.

— Micere Mugo,
Professor, poet, and playwright

Singing Your Own Praises

Marian Anderson
1897-1993

From a very young age it was clear that Marian Anderson was
gifted with an extraordinary singing voice. But when she decided
to start voice lessons, one music school in Philadelphia would
not take her because she was African-American. So Marian
began singing at parties for five dollars a show, and her church
choir raised the rest of the money to pay for private lessons.
She eventually became a famous singer, performing to crowds
in Europe and the United States who were captivated and
deeply moved by her voice. Yet even with all her achievements,
Marian still faced challenges. Racial segregation made it
impossible for her to sing with an opera company. Then,
when her agent tried to book a concert at a hall that was
the headquarters of a group called the Daughters of the
American Revolution, the group denied Marian access because
of her race. First lady, Eleanor Roosevelt, stuck up for Marian
by criticizing the DAR's racist decision. She then helped Marian
plan a concert at the Lincoln Memorial, which was enjoyed by
millions of people in person and over the radio. Finally, in 1955,
Marian joined the Metropolitan Opera, breaking a long-standing
barrier for African-Americans and inspiring many young black
vocalists. She also created a scholarship that helps young
African-American singers pay for their music studies.

 STAR QUALITIES: Gifted,
Composed, Tolerant

Thinking Beyond Today

Ada Augusta Byron, Lady Lovelace
1815-1852

What if someone told you that the first person to create a computer program was a women who lived in the early 1800's, over a hundred years before the computer revolution? Would you believe them? Well, meet Ada Augusta Byron. After her parents, the famous English poet, George Gordon, Lord Byron and Anna Isabella Millbanke Byron, separated, Ada's mother steered her studies in the direction of mathematics and science, which Ada showed an immediate passion for. Mary Somerville, the first female member of the Royal Astronomical Society, became her tutor and role model, which further encouraged Ada's math studies. When she was 18, Ada met a professor of mathematics named Charles Babbage and learned about his ideas for a machine that he called the Analytical Engine. Charles asked Ada to translate and interpret a paper he had written about the Analytical Engine. Ada not only translated the paper, but wrote a series of notes that were three times as long as Charles' original paper! In them, she outlined complex instructions for the operation of and uses for the machine. These are considered the world's first computer program. Remarkably, she also correctly predicted the future development of computer graphics, artificial intelligence, and computer-generated music. Historians have been slow to recognize Ada's genius and amazing contributions, but she is now credited with some of the earliest pioneer work in computing. In 1979, the United States Department of Defense honored her by naming a computer programming language ADA.

 STAR QUALITIES: Visionary, Enthusiastic, Optimistic

This life is yours
Take the power
to choose what you want to do
and do it well

— Susan Polis Schutz,
Poet and publisher

*We must have perseverance and above all
confidence in ourselves. We must believe that
we are gifted for something and that this
thing must be attained.*

— Marie Curie,
Polish-born French chemist and physicist

Taking Charge

Hatchepsut
1500–1460 B.C.

It is believed that while the pharaoh, Tuthmosis II,
was the official ruler of Egypt, his wife, Hatchepsut,
was actually the real power behind the scenes. When
Tuthmosis II died, his son became heir to the
throne and Hatchepsut was appointed as the young
boy's guardian. She became acting regent of the
government, but her plans apparently did not end
there. She defied tradition by declaring herself
pharaoh and dressing in the typically male dress
of a pharaoh. Hatchepsut proved to be one of
the most outstanding leaders to ever rule Egypt.
She brought peace and prosperity to the land,
facilitated an unprecedented level of foreign trade
and exploration, and helped the arts and architecture
flourish. Even after her regency should have ended
her rule, the Egyptians kept her as their pharaoh
for over 20 more years.

 STAR QUALITIES: Headstrong,
Peace-loving, Powerful

Climbing to New Heights

Junko Tabei
1939-

Junko Tabei grew up in Japan and first became interested in climbing mountains at age 10 when she climbed Mt. Nasu on a field trip with one of her teachers. She enjoyed the beauty and freshness of the mountains and liked that she could climb at her own pace. After she graduated from Showa Women's University in 1962, she began serious mountain climbing again. Junko joined climbing clubs but found that the men in the clubs would not climb with a woman. So in 1969, she created the Ladies Climbing Club of Japan, and in 1975 she led an all-female, all-Japanese expedition to the highest mountain in the world, Mt. Everest. The group faced many challenges, even a huge avalanche, but Junko kept climbing toward the top. Finally, though bruised and battered by the extreme conditions, Junko became the first woman in the world to reach the summit of Mt. Everest. Even this accomplishment was not enough to satisfy Junko; she also achieved her goal of becoming the first woman to make it to the top of the highest peak in each continent, or the "Seven Summits." Today Junko works to help preserve mountain environments from the destructive impact of climbers.

 STAR QUALITIES: Adventurous, Conscientious, Tireless

My Favorite Girls Who Grew Up Great:

_____
_____
_____
_____
_____
_____
_____
_____
_____
_____
_____
_____
_____

What I Plan to Do When I Grow Up Great

(starting right now):

_____
_____
_____
_____
_____
_____
_____
_____
_____
_____
_____
_____
_____

My Star Qualities
(not to brag or anything):

_____
_____
_____
_____
_____
_____
_____
_____
_____
_____
_____
_____
_____

Women in My Life Who Are
Girls Who Grew Up Great:

_____
_____
_____
_____
_____
_____
_____
_____
_____
_____

ACKNOWLEDGMENTS

We gratefully acknowledge the permission granted by the following authors, publishers, and authors' representatives to reprint poems or excerpts from their publications.

Harvard University Press, Cambridge, Mass., for "All serious daring starts..." from ONE WRITER'S BEGINNINGS by Eudora Welty, p. 99. Copyright © 1983, 1984 by Eudora Welty. All rights reserved.

Jonathan Clowes Ltd., London, for "There is a great line of women..." by Doris Lessing. Copyright © 1973 by Doris Lessing. Reprinted by kind permission of Jonathan Clowes, Ltd., on behalf of Doris Lessing. All rights reserved.

Rosalind Andrews-Worthy for "Listen and learn from those...." Copyright © 2003 by Rosalind Andrews-Worthy. All rights reserved.

Marian Reiner for "Thumbprint" from A SKY FULL OF POEMS by Eve Merriam, published by Random House, Inc. Copyright © 1964, 1970, 1973 by Eve Merriam. All rights reserved.

Zilpha Keatley Snyder for "To Dark Eyes Dreaming." Copyright © 1970 by Zilpha Keatley Snyder. All rights reserved.

The Children's Defense Fund for "If you don't like the way the world is..." by Marian Wright Edelman. Copyright © 1987 by Marian Wright Edelman. All rights reserved.

Weigl Educational Publishers for "Everything I have achieved..." by Natalia Makarova from VISUAL & PERFORMING ARTISTS, edited by Shaun Hunter. Copyright © 1999 by Weigl Educational Publishers Limited. All rights reserved.

Scholastic, Inc., for "I wear many blues" by Cara Rabin from MOVIN', edited by Dave Johnson in association with The New York Public Library and Poets House. Copyright © 2000 by The New York Public Library, Astor, Lenox, and Tilden Foundations. All rights reserved.

William Morris Agency for "Adults often don't understand..." by Lauren Hutton from 33 THINGS EVERY GIRL SHOULD KNOW, edited by Tonya Bolden, published by Random House, Inc. Copyright © 1998 by Tonya Bolden. All rights reserved.

Mary Frances Berry for "The time when you need to do something...." Copyright © 2002 by Mary Frances Berry. All rights reserved.

The Houston Comets as representatives of Sheryl Swoopes for "Always try to show..." by Sheryl Swoopes from LAWS OF THE BANDIT QUEENS by Ali Smith, published by Three Rivers Press. Copyright © 2002 by Ali Smith. All rights reserved.

Artists' Agency for "That's what being young is..." by Ruby Dee from I DREAM A WORLD, edited by Brian Lanker, published by Stewart, Tabori & Chang. Copyright © 1989 by Brian Lanker. All rights reserved.

Kenton S. Edelin as representative of Rebecca Lobo for "Once you know what is right and wrong..." by Rebecca Lobo from 33 THINGS EVERY GIRL SHOULD KNOW, edited by Tonya Bolden, published by Random House, Inc. Copyright © 1998 by Tonya Bolden. All rights reserved.

CMG Worldwide, Inc., www.cmgww.com, for "Adventure is worthwhile..." by Amelia Earhart. Trademark Amelia Earhart licensed by CMG Worldwide, Inc. All rights reserved.

Alfred A. Knopf, a division of Random House, Inc., and the Penguin Group UK Limited for "How wonderful it is that nobody need..." from ANNE FRANK: A DIARY OF A YOUNG GIRL. Copyright © 1994 by Alfred A. Knopf. All rights reserved.

Alfred A. Knopf, a division of Random House, Inc., for "I am doing something I learned early..." from THE GOLD CELL by Sharon Olds. Copyright © 1987 by Sharon Olds. All rights reserved.

Julie O'Callaghan for "Surfboard Life." Copyright © 1998 by Julie O'Callaghan. All rights reserved.

Girls Incorporated for "The Girls Inc. Girls' Bill of Rights." Copyright © 1992 by Girls Incorporated. All rights reserved.

Harcourt, Inc., and Curtis Brown, Ltd., for "Wanda Gág" from HERSELF by Ann Whitford Paul. Copyright © 1999 by Ann Whitford Paul. All rights reserved.

Curtis Brown, Ltd., for "Girls Can, Too!" from GIRLS CAN TOO! A Book of Poems by Lee Bennett Hopkins, published by Franklin Watts, Inc. Copyright © 1972 by Lee Bennett Hopkins. All rights reserved.

Micere Mugo for "Where are those songs?" Copyright © 2002 by Micere Mugo. All rights reserved.

Musée Curie for "We must have perseverance..." by Marie Curie. Copyright © by Musée Curie. All rights reserved.

A careful effort has been made to trace the ownership of selections used in this anthology in order to obtain permission to reprint copyrighted material and give proper credit to the copyright owners. If any error or omission has occurred, it is completely inadvertent, and we would like to make corrections in future editions provided that written notification is made to the publisher:

BLUE MOUNTAIN ARTS, INC., P.O. Box 4549, Boulder, Colorado 80306.